Blackburn

in old picture postcards

by
Peter Worden
and
Robin Whalley

European Library - Zaltbommel/Netherlands MCMLXXXIV

GB ISBN 90 288 2892 3

European Library in Zaltbommel/Netherlands publishes among other things the following series:

IN OLD PICTURE POSTCARDS *is a series of books which sets out to show what a particular place looked like and what life was like in Victorian and Edwardian times. A book about virtually every town in the United Kingdom is to be published in this series. By the end of this year about 175 different volumes will have appeared. 1,250 books have already been published devoted to the Netherlands with the title* **In oude ansichten.** *In Germany, Austria and Switzerland 500, 60 and 15 books have been published as* **In alten Ansichten;** *in France by the name* **En cartes postales anciennes** *and in Belgium as* **En cartes postales anciennes** *and/or* **In oude prentkaarten** *150 respectively 400 volumes have been published.*

For further particulars about published or forthcoming books, apply to your bookseller or direct to the publisher.

This edition has been printed and bound by Grafisch Bedrijf De Steigerpoort in Zaltbommel/Netherlands.

INTRODUCTION

This portrayal of Blackburn in Victorian and Edwardian times, and onwards until 1930, has no higher aim than to be a nostalgic trip down memory lane. Particular emphasis has been placed on scenes which have changed, buildings which have been demolished and characters long since deceased. Whilst some redevelopment of the outmoded Victorian fabric was inevitable, many people lament that so much of our heritage has been lost.

These years saw Blackburn at the peak of urban growth and importance. The cotton famine of the 1860's had ended. There was a feeling throughout the textile industry of euphoric optimism at the prospect of ever-expanding overseas markets. In 1901, with no unemployment, the prosperity of the cotton trade was reflected in the briskness of every branch of the local economy.

Throughout the pre-1914 period mill building continued apace. After the First World War came another boom in the cotton trade. Blackburn was the world's greatest weaving centre. More than 140 mills, with 100,000+ looms, produced over a mile of cloth every twenty seconds. As four-fifths was exported Blackburn was known worldwide. The whirlpool of disaster still lay hidden beneath the calm waters of prosperity.

Civic pride knew no bounds as an almost profligate programme of expansive municipal building activity was undertaken. Vast unseen, or at best quickly taken-for-granted, public works were carried through as sewers, roads and bridges were built.

The new railway station, opened in 1888, was the hub of six radial routes. The Leeds and Liverpool Canal continued to carry large quantities of goods, fuel and raw materials. Trams were introduced in the 1880's, originally steam or horse drawn; the electrification programme commenced in 1898. Motor bus operations began in Blackburn in 1920 and the Corporation omnibus service started at the end of the decade.

Cotton manufacturing dominated the social and economic life of Blackburn for three centuries. By 1650 the town had become well known for its blue and white 'Blackburn Checks' and soon afterwards for 'Blackburn Greys'. Many cottages had handlooms, the weaver producing the cotton pieces in his own time. In the eighteenth and early nineteenth centuries a succession of inventions revolutionised textiles. The essentially cottage based industry gave way, not always peacefully, to a highly mechanised factory system.

In 1768, shortly after he moved from Stanhill, James Hargreaves' house at Ramsclough was ransacked by a mob who saw his newly invented 'Spinning Jenny' as a threat to their livelihoods. Blackburn saw further 'popular unrest' (riots!) with the introduction of powerlooms in 1826 and again in 1842 and 1878.

The town grew out of all recognition. The population, under 12,000 in 1801, had reached 46,000 in 1851 when the town became a Municipal Borough. By 1881 it had more than doubled to over 104,000 and twenty years later was almost 130,000.

The cotton industry gave employment to most; smaller numbers were engaged in flour mills, engineering works producing textile machinery, coachbuilding and the breweries. Blackburn was noted for 'a pub on every corner'!

In 1870 the Post Office introduced the first British postcard. Its monopoly prevented picture postcard development until 1894 when privately printed postcards for use with adhesive stamps were permitted. Until 1897 no message was allowed on the address side, the picture on the front being reduced to leave space for the message. In 1902, with the introduction of the 'divided back' card — one half used for the message and the other used for the address —, the picture postcard settled into the format we know today.

The first two decades of this century saw a phenomenal postcard boom. The family postcard album became a status symbol and the craze for collecting was frantic. Millions of cards were produced, bought and eagerly posted. Some were sent without a message, or simply 'sent in affection to swell your collection'.

The cards, mostly costing 1d. each and with postage unchanged at Äd. until doubled in 1918, occupied the role of the telephone of today. Postcards were used as message carriers within the town; for example: 'Can you play for us on Saturdayü' Up to three million cards a day were posted in Britain. The efficiency of the postal service was reflected in messages which frequently referred to meetings later the same day, such as: 'Dear Alice, coming tonight, with love Flo.'

One of the fascinations of old postcards today is the messages themselves, sometimes poignant, sometimes comical. Local examples include a card dated November 1917: 'Dear Jinnie, It was only too true over our Dick, we got official news last Tuesday.' Alternatively, a concerned A.A. Gregory once wrote: 'Dear Aunt and Uncle. Our Willie has heard that your Willie has got bit with a dog. Hoping it is not serious.'

The weather was, as ever, a topic of conversation with the rain frequently 'putting a damper on everything'. A favourite message on a card showing the Northern Daily Telegraph building reads: 'Dear Flo. We are having rare larks here. The big building is where Ted is. I am worrying about my box which hasn't arrived yet. Buck up. It has rained every day.

Love Beatrice.' Not everyone, though, was satisfied. Writing home to Norfolk in 1912, one man said: 'Having a good time here, lovely weather. I think this is about the dirtiest town I ever saw.'

Most of the pictures included are from 'real photograph' postcards. Apart from having finer quality than the mass-produced printed cards, they were often the only type of picture postcard which could be produced by local photographers on a shoestring. 'Try one dozen. Send your Photo. Work guaranteed.'

Old photographs are subject to image fading and precipitation of silver salts which causes the surface to take on a mirror-like glaze. Where this has happened they have been painstakingly restored by Roland Whiteside to give them this new lease of life.

It would be remiss not to thank, for their help and advice in the preparation of this book, Brian Darbyshire (District Librarian) and Stanley Miller (Local History Assistant) of the Blackburn Central Library, and Adrian Lewis (Arts and Museums Manager) and Michael Millward (Curator) of Blackburn Museum and Art Gallery.

Equally, while much of the material is from our own collections, we should not forget those who have contributed from their own sources, or 'pointed us in the right direction', amongst whom we must mention: Edward Buckle, Robert Fergusson, David Frankland, George Hall, Mavis Harrison, Margaret Haydock, Frank and Frances Higgins, Margaret Hodgson, Susan Jackson, Arthur Newell, Colin Reilly, Ray Smith, Mike Sumner, and Mary Whalley.

In the end we could have filled a book twice this size!

1. The Cathedral features prominently on this fine aerial view taken on a market day in 1930. The Town Hall is in the top left hand corner. To the right of the market place, roads radiate from Salford Bridge. In the foreground is Darwen Street; leading to the Boulevard is Jubilee Street with the Grand and Palace Theatres in view.

Blackburn. Parish Church.

2. *Parish Church 1905.* Blackburn's ancient Parish Church, dedicated to St. Mary, has probably existed since Saxon times. The foundation stone of the present Gothic edifice, designed by John Palmer, was laid by Vicar T.D. Whitaker on 2nd September 1820 and the building consecrated on 13th September 1826. To make way for it, the old church which had stood to the left of the photograph and the small, dark Tudor Grammar School were demolished. Services were transferred to St. John's and the Grammar School moved to new premises in Bull Meadow, Freckleton Street. The Parish Church School, opened in 1871, can be seen on the right.

INTERIOR OF BLACKBURN CATHEDRAL.

3. *Blackburn Cathedral 1930*. The new Diocese of Blackburn came into being in November 1926. This view of the interior of the Cathedral – as it had now become – was taken shortly afterwards. The necessary extensions to fit it for its new purpose were begun in 1938. Few people could then have realised that completion would take thirty years. The galleries were removed, so giving the nave a renewed airiness. The East Window, a fine example of Flemish glass, had been brought from Belgium by the Vicar Dr. J.W. Whittaker in 1826; part is now incorporated in the new fabric as the North Window.

4. *Blackburn Station 1905.* Blackburn entered the railway age on Whit Monday, 1st June 1846 when the line to Preston was opened to passengers. It had taken two years to build under the supervision of resident engineer Terence Woulf Flanagan; a central station was built on land known as Stonybutts for £6,309. According to one account 'the pleasure of the day was much enhanced by the fact that no accident occurred to cast a gloom over the proceedings'. During the next four years lines were constructed to Bolton, Chatburn and Colne. The so-called Darwen Street (Nova Scotia) Station of the Blackburn, Darwen and Bolton Railway Company was used from 1848 to 1852, when agreement was reached to use the L. & Y.'s more convenient location.

Station Front, Blackburn

5. *Station Front 1910.* By the 1880's Blackburn's original central station had become severely congested, a fact dramatically brought into focus on the 8th August 1881 when it was the scene of one of the worst accidents ever on the Lancashire and Yorkshire Railway. Seven people were killed and thirty injured when the Manchester to Hellifield express ran at speed into a shunting engine, primarily due to inadequate signalling. Construction of the present station commenced in June 1885, the contract being awarded to Robert Neill and Sons for £53,233, and the opening was in March 1888. To complement this new structure, Salford Bridge and Railway Road were widened, the Blakewater culverted, and the marshy waste turned into a handsome esplanade – the Boulevard.

6. *Boulevard 1905*. Only the wealthy owned their own carriages and until the 1880's 'shank's pony' was the usual mode of travel for the majority. Horse drawn buses operated a limited service within the town. In 1881 the Blackburn and Over Darwen Tramways Company began a steam tram service between the two towns. Five years later the Blackburn Corporation Tramways Company started construction of routes to Church, the Cemetery, Billinge End and Witton, which were opened by the end of the decade. These services were augmented by a fleet of privately owned hansom-cabs and four-wheeled 'growlers', seen here at the cab stands outside the railway station. In the background work has begun on the foundations for Queen Victoria's statue.

7. *Boulevard 1930*. Twenty-five years later the scene has changed considerably. Electrification of the tramways had begun in 1898 and over the next decade the lines were extended to Queen's Park, Cherry Tree and Wilpshire. Motorbus operation began in the town in 1920 with a service to Rishton by Kenyon, Coleman and Robinson. One of their char-a-bancs can be seen parked, second from the left, ready to drive people into the countryside on this sunny summer afternoon. Among the first to offer local services was the Blackburn Bus Company. One of its Leyland 'G' types can be seen in the foreground. Blackburn Corporation omnibuses entered service in November 1929 and they acquired the Blackburn Bus Company's routes in March 1931.

8. *Railway Road circa 1920.* Hepworth's store later became the Corporation Tramways offices; by that time Woolworth's were occupying a smaller adjoining shop, before later taking over the site. To the right is New Water Street. In front of these buildings, thirty years earlier, the steam tram shown opposite had stood. In the distance is the Theatre Royal. A 'New Theatre' existed near the Ainsworth Street site of the Theatre Royal in 1787. The building fell into disrepair and in 1818 was replaced by a more substantial 'Theatre Royal and Opera House'. This was renovated in 1867, and rebuilt twenty years later with Frank Matcham as architect. It became a cinema in 1931. The well-remembered cream tiled façade disappeared in 1967.

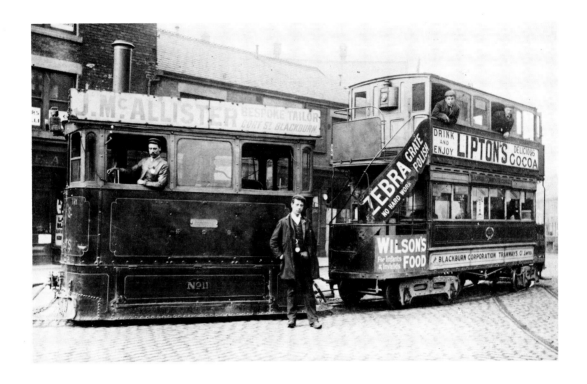

9. *Salford Bridge Terminus circa 1897.* The Corporation's preference was for horse tramways through-out the town. However, the firm which undertook both to construct and operate the tramways on the town's behalf would only do so if it could also use steam power. To work the nine miles of tramway seventy horses, eight open top cars, fifteen steam engines and nineteen passenger trailers were acquired. Seen here, liberally daubed with advertisements, are Messrs. Green's engine No. 11 towing car No. 13 made by the Falcon Company. Although offering an improved ride compared with the horse buses, the steam trams as they grew older failed to comply with the regulations requiring that they be quiet and consume their own smoke.

10. *Salford circa 1910.* In the early years of the nineteenth century Salford Bridge was a veritable bottleneck. It was only fifteen feet wide, extremely humpbacked and hemmed in by adjacent property. It was first widened in 1846 but not until forty years later was the vast open space shown above created. Although the property on either side of Holme Street has now gone, the fine gabled buildings fronting Railway Road still remain. Between Thomas Cook's 'tourist excursion and shipping office' and the offices of the Great Northern Railway can be seen Boyle's confectioner's shop. James Boyle — or 'Toffy Jem' as he was known — is probably best remembered for his Jap Nuggets.

11. *Church Street 1903*. As part of the road widening schemes the Bay Horse and the Lord Nelson public houses were set back some fifty feet and re-erected in the substantial early Victorian style. An open-topped tram is waiting at the Wilpshire terminus. The buildings on the left have now been redeveloped. The Central Fish Emporium also sold rabbit and game; Cowburn's manufactured umbrellas and walking sticks. Next door was Astley's, stationers and booksellers, the walls plastered with advertising plaques for 'Lion's Ink' and various newspapers. The postcard was sent by a young girl who had recently moved from Fleetwood to the Bay Horse, and she tells her friend she likes 'living at Blackburn very well'.

12. *Salford 1879.* Few will recognise this view of Salford with Starkie Street Foundry behind, as the shops were demolished shortly after 1879. From the left, the shopkeepers were: Mrs. Margaret Boylan, confectioner; James McCloud, earthenware dealer; Thomas Harvey Chastney, picture framer; and John Cook's clothes shop has already closed. The irregularity of the buildings was typical of the haphazard pattern of construction in years gone by. Only Nancy Leach's 'Peel's Arms' remains today; no longer a public house, it was for many years occupied by Rice's printers.

13. *Salford 1879.* This view of Salford looking from Foundry Hill towards Penny Street is unrecognisable today but it captures the spirit of the age – cobbled and unmade streets and the reliance on horse-drawn transportation. Along with special offers on butter and cheese, resulting from a Glasgow bank failure, the adverts on the left indicate the importance of ham and bacon which could be cured for longer keeping. This unhygienic display would be frowned on today. Shaw's Bow Street brewery on the left and Noblett's corn miller and provision dealer's shop on the right have long since disappeared, the latter being replaced by the Salvation Army Citadel in 1925.

Blackburn.

Church Street.

14. *Church Street circa 1905.* Gone are the days when people could casually stop and chat in the middle of the road. Gone, too, is Dr. Pollard's distinctive ivy covered house. Beyond – with the two coaches outside – stood the Golden Lion, once an important coaching inn and well known for its cellars full of hogsheads of home brewed 'best'. Boot's 'cash chemists' had arrived and were to remain in Church Street until their removal to the new shopping precinct. In the distance on Churchgate (as it used to be called) stood the old manor house, the home of the Feildens until they moved to Witton.

15. *Church Street circa 1900.* Blackburn's ancient market cross formerly stood at the junction of Darwen Street and Church Street, and this was the site of the old market place. The town's last surviving half-timbered tenements were demolished to make way for the Thwaites Arcade, seen on the left. Completed in 1883 it was named after Daniel Thwaites, the influential millionaire brewer and one time Member of Parliament. The Old Bull Hotel was an important coaching inn and after its rebuilding in 1847 it became the town's premier hostelry. The tower of the Old Parish Church stood within feet of the rear windows until 1870.

King William Street, Blackburn

16. *King William Street 1908.* When King William Street was opened in 1832 five shops, which for 350 years had stood on the north side of Church Street, and Mr. Sudell's warehouse fronting Lord Street had to be demolished. The effort was, however, worthwhile for Whittle described it twenty years later as *the noblest street in the borough... The Albert, New Market and Victoria buildings, in the vicinity of the covered market, are very lofty and elegant and reflect infinite credit upon the builders and the town.* Many people will recall Burton the Tailor's shop occupying the site of the former Prince of Wales.

17. *King William Street circa 1906.* Livesey Street, as it is named on Gillies map of 1824, used to run from Lord Street to Thunder Alley (Town Hall Street). Opposite its junction with Thunder Alley was a bowling green which would now have been directly in front of the Town Hall. Victoria Buildings, on the left of the photograph, were the home of E.H. Booth and Company for sixty-four years until they were forced to move in 1966. Two generations of transportation can be seen: in the distance, a horse-drawn four wheeled 'growler'; and in the foreground, an open-topped horseless carriage.

Victoria Street showing Market   Blackburn

18. *Victoria Street 1902.* Before Victoria Street was laid out, this short section was actually part of Ainsworth Street. On the left is the New Inn. Originally it stood at the junction with Church Street and was an old coaching inn. This link with transport continued into this century as first the trams and then the Corporation buses stopped outside. The area behind was a veritable warren of entries and passages with ancient houses almost randomly erected around two squares – Haworth Square and Old Square. Both vanished with the extension of Lord Street in 1864. The inn and the adjoining property were demolished to make way for Littlewood's store, which itself has now been engulfed by the shopping precinct.

19. *Victoria Street 1904.* By the early nineteenth century the old market place had become congested with stalls overflowing into John Fleming's New Square and Market Street Lane. In 1845 a new market place covering over two and a half acres was planned by the Improvement Commissioners alongside the proposed covered market hall. The market square was enclosed by buildings along Victoria Street after 1854. The traditional market and the specialised, independent shopkeeper were soon challenged, first by the Co-operative societies with their attractive 'divi' and then by the multiple stores, like the Maypole chain, which relied on lower profit margins but a faster turnover. The distant chimney belonged to the Corporation's old Electricity Works on Jubilee Street.

20./21. *Market Place 1900.* The extensive cobbled market place could accommodate over three hundred stalls which had to be erected and dismantled twice each week. It was also the location of the Easter fair, which had formerly been held on Blakey Moor. Tea, previously an upper class luxury, only became the national drink with the influx of Indian tea in the mid-nineteenth century. This placed the tea trade in the forefront of commercial competition. The four shops on the right all sold the popular beverage...

...These typically Victorian buildings, including the Crown Hotel on the left, and the Reform Club on the right, were built on Lower Tacketts Field which in 1832 was the scene of the first Parliamentary hustings. The Reform Club, opened in 1866, played an important part in the chequered history of Blackburn Liberalism and became a centre for social as well as political life in the town. The buildings were demolished in 1967 as part of the town centre redevelopment scheme.

22. *Bible Caravan, Market Place circa 1902.* At the turn of the century the 'terraced' caravan was a popular method of religious proselytising. The 'Luther' Protestant Van, operated by 'The Church Association and National Protestant League: Established to Maintain the Protestant Character of the Church of England' is here seen on the Hen Market, a site on Victoria Street opposite the present (sole remaining) County Court. Later built over by the wooden Wholesale Fruiterers' warehouses, it is now obliterated by the Car Park approach ramp. Note the typical high Eton collars worn by the boys, and the Independent Labour Party poster on the wall behind.

23. *Bible Caravan, Market Place circa 1902.* This slightly less grand Ebenezer Bible Carriage is here doing good business, surrounded by men and children in typical dress — all the children wear clogs. In the background can be seen part of Lord Street — the Grosvenor Hotel and the entrance block to Thwaites Arcade, with its cast iron swing-crane attached to the wall. Note the stick and hoop carried by the boy, and the traditional shawl attire — now becoming obsolete — worn by the girl. This effective way of 'preaching the gospel' was later adopted by the Socialist Party with its National Clarion Van in 1914.

24. *Town Hall, foundation stone laying ceremony 1852.* This early photograph shows Joseph Feilden, Lord of the Manor, laying the foundation stone of the Town Hall on October 28th, 1852. As major landowners and later millowners, the Feilden family's history is inextricably linked with that of the town. They often contributed to deserving causes: local schools, churches and hospitals benefitted from their generosity. Joseph Feilden was Deputy Lieutenant of Lancashire and was also the first Justice of the Peace in Blackburn. At the age of 73 he entered politics and was one of the town's two Members of Parliament for four years before his death in 1870.

25. *Town Hall 1905.* The Town Hall was opened on October 30th, 1856 by the Mayor, William Hoole. In addition to an assembly room, council chamber and offices, the building originally housed the court, police offices and cells with the Chief Constable's house at the rear. The architect of this dignified, well proportioned building was James Paterson and the contractors were Richard Hacking and William Stones. 'Dickie' Hacking, a well known, conscientious man, often preferred to lose money rather than spoil a structure with shoddy workmanship. He lost money in building the Town Hall, as the outbreak of the Crimean War resulted in a sharp rise in the price of materials.

KING WILLIAM STREET, BLACKBURN.

10036-11

26. *King William Street 1914*. In the centre are the Peel Buildings, erected in 1854, and named after the former Prime Minister Sir Robert Peel whose statue can be seen on the roof. The Peel family was the most successful of the pioneers of both cotton manufacture and calico printing in the Blackburn area. Unfortunately the statue was demolished on August 10th, 1934 when the site was redeveloped by Marks and Spencer. By 1919 Furness' drapers had occupied over half the block on acquiring Worswick's premises. Cornelius Hall, 'silk mercer and fancy draper', whose shop was in Town Hall Street, reputedly had the most superbly dressed windows in the town.

27. *Market Place 1910.* The Market Hall was designed by Terence Flanagan, the resident engineer of the Blackburn and Preston Railway Company. The wrought iron roof supports, considered daring at the time, were manufactured at William Yates' foundry. It opened on 28th January 1848 and the adjoining Fish Market was added in 1872. The Market Hall is fondly remembered for its eighteen foot square, seventy-two foot high campanile Tower which was capped by a golden ball which rose on its staff at Noon and descended at One. This was the cue for the town's One o'clock gun, which was last fired on New Year's Eve 1931. The tower came to an ignominious end, being demolished on 30th December 1964.

28. *Open Market Place circa 1905.* It is uncertain when Blackburn's market was first established, but by 1651 the town had 'a great weekly market for cattle, corn and provisions'. Two hundred years later, according to Whittle, the new open market included 'Californian pea stands and butchers' stalls' whilst others sold 'hot black puddings, fruit, cheese, potatoes, vegetables, pots, china and earthenware'. The rent for a twenty-four foot fruit stall was then 4d., compared with a butcher's stall at one shilling. Here, beside the Town Hall, Market Superintendent John Charles Houghton (on the left in the peaked cap) oversees this delightfully posed transaction.

29. *Tomlinson's Christmas Show 1934.* When the Market Hall opened the stall holders included 'butchers, confectioners, booksellers, milliners, greengrocers, poulterers, tripe and cow heel dealers, clog makers and bonnet dealers'. Whittle also informs us that 'On Saturday, 20th December 1851, Christmas time, the various butchers' shops and stalls had a fine display of beef and pork, such a display, indeed, as we have rarely witnessed before at the corresponding season of the year.' Geese were also plentiful, and sold at 7d. per pound! The adjoining fishmarket's interior changed little over the years and the traditional Christmas displays continued. Tomlinson's sold only the best and reputedly charged a few coppers more. The business moved to the New Markets in November 1964.

Blackburn. The Exchange.

30. *Blackburn Exchange circa 1905*. A considerable trade in cotton yarn developed between the weaving town of Blackburn, and Manchester and the surrounding spinning towns. A weekly Wednesday yarn market was established. In 1852 business was transacted in the open street opposite the Bull Inn in the midst of noise and confusion on market day. The corner stone of the Exchange was laid on March 10th, 1863 by the Mayor J.B.S. Sturdy and opened in April 1865. Only part of William Brakspear's design was ever built. Outside 'change hours the premises were used for public meetings and concerts, soon becoming the main centre of live entertainment in the town. Following internal alterations it opened as the New Majestic Cinema in March 1924.

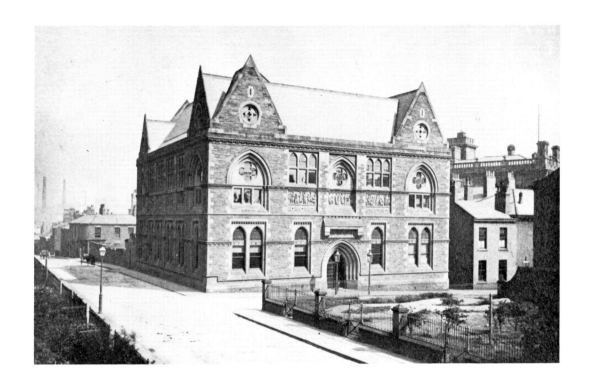

31. *Public Free Library and Museum circa 1890.* The Town Council decided in 1853 to adopt the provisions of the Public Free Libraries Act. The Library opened, with local historian W.A. Abram as Librarian, in rooms in the Town Hall in February 1862. The fine building illustrated was designed by Messrs. Woodzell and Collcutt to have imposing frontages to Frances (then Library, now Museum) Street and Richmond Terrace. Under the first floor windows are sculptured panels representing Art, Literature, Science, Agriculture, Iron Manufactures, Cotton Manufactures and Commerce. The corner stone was laid on July 18th, 1872 and it was opened on June 11th, 1874. It is seen here before the now demolished School Board Offices were built opposite.

Blackburn. Technical School.

32. *Technical School circa 1905*. Plans were established for its institution as a Jubilee memorial in 1887 and a subscription fund of £15,000 was raised. The foundation stone was laid with Masonic honours by H.R.H. the Prince of Wales (later Edward VII) on 9th May 1888, the town being 'en fête' for the occasion. Building operations began the following year. Some classes were held in 1891 but it was not until the end of 1894 that construction was completed. The lavishly decorated nine-bay front is of red and buff Ruabon pressed brick, with buff terracotta dressing. This fine building, recently in danger of demolition, has fortunately been renovated. On the right is the now demolished tower of St. Paul's School, built in 1858.

33. *Y.M.C.A., Limbrick 1908.* The foundation stone of the new premises in Limbrick for the Young Men's Christian Association was laid by Lord Kinnaird, President of the National Council of the Y.M.C.A. on 9th May 1908. The architect of this handsome building was Mr. F.J. Parkinson whose offices were close by on Richmond Terrace. It was opened on 21st July 1910 by Councillor Scholes Rostron. The original drawing contained two (never built) shops, one on either side of the main entrance, and a lecture hall which was later converted into a theatre. A fire in August 1964 made the building unusable. The Y.M.C.A. moved to Shear Bank Road, and the premises reopened in November 1968 as the 'Sir Charles Napier', replacing the former inn just visible on the other side of Tontine Street.

34. *Northgate circa 1909.* This view of Northgate, with the corner of Duke Street on the right, shows the buildings which existed prior to the construction of the Sessions House. A long drawn out controversy preceded its erection and over £80,000 was paid for the land, property and goodwill of the site. The Blakey Moor area had seen better days; some houses were originally local cotton manufacturers' mansions. In 1891 it had been described as a *mass of poor and squalid property. A triangular shaped area of mean looking tenements including within it the salubrious localities of Cannon Street and Engine Street. A good proportion of the property is in a dilapidated condition; it abounds in tramps' lodgings and houses of an even worse description.*

THE NEW PUBLIC BUILDINGS NORTHGATE BLACKBURN. 1912

35. *Sessions House, Northgate 1912.* The new Police Station and Sessions House was necessary as the Police had outgrown their premises at the rear of the Town Hall, premises which were subsequently demolished and the Town Hall extended. Built of Butler Delph stone at a cost of nearly £47,000, it was formally opened by Sir Harry Hornby on July 25th, 1912; the same day Lord Morley and Sir William Coddington received the Freedom of the Borough. The two huge figures of Justice and Mercy can be seen over the main entrances. In the distance are the buildings which then occupied the site of the Public Halls, the foundation stone of which was not laid until the following year.

36. *Preston New Road 1903.* When the new Blackburn to Preston Turnpike road was opened in 1826, it not only cut the journey between the two towns by over two miles but followed a less arduous route. The bottom of Preston New Road, close to its junction with Sudell Cross, has changed little in the last eighty years. The spire of St. George's Presbyterian Church can be seen on the left. Built in 1865-1868 for the use of the majority of the original United Presbyterians in the town, it is the only building in view to have been demolished. The garden fronts of the houses on the right and the lamp standards have also disappeared.

37. *Preston New Road circa 1904.* This delightful view, so vibrant with detail and quite unposed, really conveys the feeling of eighty years ago. In the distance are two horse-drawn vehicles: the front one a soil-cart, and the rear one a flat-truck loaded with crates. A small boy pushes a little hand cart in the middle of the road. The central tramway standards, with their protective bollards (each bearing the town's coat of arms on both sides) were very soon to be replaced by the much plainer kerb-edge variety. Note the street-lighting units half way up each standard.

Billings End, Blackburn

38. *Billinge End circa 1910.* Billinge End was the location of the first toll bar on the new road to Preston until 1843 when it was replaced by the one at Shackerley. Many people used to cycle daily from the surrounding countryside to Billinge End to catch a tram into town. They would leave their bicycles at Ivy Cottages, where they would be looked after for a few coppers per week. Twelve of these single deck trams were purchased and they were often decorated on special occasions. Less powerful than the double deck cars, they were the first to be disposed of in 1938. The rustic cabin, on the left, was later resited across the road and remained there for many years, though the cottages were demolished in the 1930's.

39. *Billinge End circa 1905.* An extensive forest once stretched from Revidge almost to the Ribble and was preserved as a Royal Chase. Revidge Road was constructed, in 1826, under the direction of the famous road maker John McAdam. It was one of a number of relief measures to alleviate the distress and find work for the starving weavers. Just off Revidge Road, on the right, was the Mile End handloom weaving colony where as late as 1851, three-quarters of those in employment were still engaged in handloom weaving. The bricked-up cellar loomshop windows can still be seen today. Billinge Sunday School, built in 1834, superseded a school held in an upper room of a cottage in Dinkley Square.

Blackburn. St. Silas's Church.

40. *St. Silas' Church circa 1905*. In 1846 the Billinge Sunday School (now the Parish Centre) was licenced for worship as a Chapel of Ease to St. Paul's Church. Thirty years later, as the district was developing, the idea of a new church was promoted and the site given and enclosed. However, it was not until 8th December 1894 that Mrs. Tattersall, of Quarry Bank, Billinge End Road, laid the foundation stone. The church, designed by Messrs. Paley and Austin of Lancaster, opened for Divine Service on Ascension Day, 9th May 1898. The porch, baptistry and tower, the latter devoid of its intended spire, were not added until 1913. The house Fair Elms (on the left) was later demolished to make way for the vicarage.

41. *Dukes Brow 1904*. Dukes Brow, seen here from Gibraltar Street, is one of the oldest roads leading into the town and before the construction of Preston New Road was also one of the most important. Its name is derived from a farmer, James Whalley, who during the Civil War resided at Bank House and was known as the 'Duke of the Bank'. Bank House, close to the junction of Dukes Brow and Adelaide Terrace, is one of the oldest houses in Blackburn. Later occupants included Dr. Barlow and 'Jackie' Smith, master mason and ex-mayor. It is interesting to note how few of the houses on the right then had gardens, and the trees on the left have long since gone.

42. *Lynwood Road circa 1905*. These terraced houses are typical of those built around the turn of the century as the town's rapid expansion continued. This view at the junction with Higher Bank Street shows the road as yet unmade, and was taken before Leamington Road Baptist Sunday School was extended in 1911. Later at Number 57, behind the lamp, lived the contralto Kathleen Ferrier who in her early twenties began singing at local concerts. Her potential was recognised after she was chosen as the best singer at the Carlisle Festival. Moving to London in 1942, she soon acquired an international reputation, but a promising career was cut short by her untimely death from cancer in October 1953. Many recordings survive as testimony to her unique voice.

43. *New Bank Road 1905*. 'Fierce conflagration in Granville Road' was the headline in the Blackburn Times following the fire on Tuesday November 14th, 1905 at the boot and shoe shop of Mr. William Sheffield. The fire which started in the shop quickly spread to the rest of the house. The horse-drawn fire engine took eleven minutes to arrive; which, considering it was 'collar work' all the way, was regarded as a remarkably good time. Although the fire was soon under control, Mr. Sheffield and his family were rendered homeless, all their furniture and his large stock of boots and shoes being reduced to ashes. It is amazing that this picture had been made into a postcard, bought and posted within forty-eight hours of the fire.

FIRE AT WILLAN & MILLS FOUNDRY, BLACKBURN. MAY 6. 1909.

44. *Willan and Mills Fire 1909.* More than 20,000 people flocked to see the spectacular timber fire on the evening of May 6th, 1909 at the former Willan and Mills foundry on Higher Audley Street. The fire spread quickly, fanned by a strong wind. The full strength of the Fire Brigade, three engines, was called out. The firemen had the fire under control surprisingly quickly but not before considerable damage was done to the large joiners' shop and the adjacent houses in Chester Street. Damping-down operations continued the next day, and this fireman certainly seems relieved that the blaze is out.

45. *Church Street Flood 1901*. The normally insignificant River Blakewater overflowed its banks on November 12th, 1901. A depth of three feet six inches was recorded in Water Street, for once appropriately named. The lower auditorium of the Theatre Royal was soon inundated. Beer barrels, apple tubs, orange boxes and flotsam of a more dubious nature floated down Church Street. Mrs. Astley, trapped by the rising floodwater, had to be rescued from her newsagent's shop. A horse and cart were backed up against the shop front and a ladder placed on it, by which she descended from an upstairs window.

46. *The Big Lamp circa 1880.* The 'Big Lamp', with its four huge gas lamps dominating a horse trough, stood for many years in the centre of Sudell Cross as a memorial to the chequered years of 'Jackie' Smith's mayoralty. 'Jackie' donated it to the town, though the cost was ultimately borne by the Council when he became involved in financial difficulties. Modification of the lamps to upturned brackets followed a tragic explosion on 7th July 1882 which killed local teacher Mr. Wilkinson and injured two other passers-by.

47. *Sudell Cross circa 1890*. The Fire Engine and Lamp Committee resolved that the pedestal and standard, which had survived the explosion, should be refitted with the patent lamps and burners shown above. An entirely new replacement lamp was erected in 1892 and the horse trough was removed to Northgate. A horse-drawn tram can be seen going along King William Street. The horses were stabled next to the tramshed in Simmons Street which was approached by the branch line seen on the right.

48. *Kidder Street 20th September 1941*. The worst tram accident in Blackburn occurred as the Darwen Corporation tramcar was proceeding to Darwen along Bolton Road. At the junction with Kidder Street it jumped the points, swung to the left and overturned against Sykes' shop. The driver, Richard Webb, was killed and fourteen passengers were injured. At the inquiry the Inspector concluded that the accident was caused by a combination of the points being loose and open, and the unauthorised speed of the vehicle. 20th September was an ill-fated date for Darwen Corporation Tramways as on that day fifteen years previously a tram had run out of control down Sudell Road killing two people and injuring seven more.

49. *Trams on Train 1901*. The Corporation's desire to have the first overhead electric wire tramway in East Lancashire was to cost it dearly. £109,000 was paid to purchase the system within the Borough from the Blackburn, and the Blackburn and Over Darwen, Tramway Companies. Following the necessary Act of Parliament in 1898 another £150,000 was spent on extending and electrifying the system. The first eight electric tramcars were for use on the former horse-operated Preston New Road and Witton routes. They were built by Milnes but always known as 'Siemans' cars after the firm which supplied the electrical equipment. In 1901 these were supplemented by forty open top cars of a larger, more advanced type which arrived by rail in a partly dismantled state.

50. *Whalley New Road circa 1905.* These cars, also built by Milnes, had distinctive 'hexagonal' ends and were over thirty-four feet in length with their long vestibuled platforms. Down each side of the lower saloon was seating for sixteen and thirty-four seats were provided outside. Car 58 would have been resplendent in the familiar 'half and half' green and ivory colour scheme. The car is seen here with early features, notably the side mounted trolley mast, wire lifeguards and wooden 'decency' boards round the upper deck. The seats had been extended over the platforms but there was as yet no headlight. All the open top trams, never the most suitable in our inclement weather, were housed at the Intack depot from 1902.

51. *Intack Depot Body Shop 1927*. In 1906 four cars were fitted with enclosed top covers. The majority were not covered until after 1925 when it was discovered that the bridges could be cleared by replacing the wheels with ones of a smaller diameter. This work, which integrated so well with the existing bodywork, was completed under the supervision of body shop foreman Wilfred Rossall. Ironically, the remaining open-top cars often appeared in winter, since their larger wheels kept the motors clear of the snow. The unremunerative Audley section was the first to close in 1935. The inevitable end, although delayed by the War, came on 3rd September 1949 when the last tram, illuminated for the occasion, climbed its way from the Boulevard to Intack.

52. *Rowland Baguley & Co, Shuttle Works, Addison Street circa 1920.* Rowland Baguley began manufacturing shuttles in 1840. The business prospered, and the firm twice moved into larger premises. The management of the firm eventually passed to his son-in-law John Duckworth, who later became an Alderman of the Borough. Shortly after he took control, the company bought the Addison Street Works, a former cotton weaving shed. Their shuttles, made principally from Cornelwood (Dogwood), Persimmon, and African Boxwood, were exported worldwide. The sample racks contained several thousand shuttles, each exhibiting slight differences and showing the minute variations necessary to weave the multitudinous varieties of textile fabrics. The firm ceased production around 1930 and the site is now occupied by the Zion Pentecostal Church.

53. *Holehouse Mill circa 1905.* Child labour, especially the use of pauper apprentices from the Workhouses, was an evil which concerned the early reformers. By 1850 no child under 8 years was allowed to work; up to 13 years they could only work 6½ hours a day and had to receive 10 hours education weekly. Women and children aged 13 to 18 were forbidden to work more than 10 hours daily or 58 hours a week. In 1874 the minimum age was raised to 10 and workers aged 10 to 14 years had to attend school 'half-time'. Manufacturers employed separate morning and afternoon shifts of half-timers to maintain production. By 1901 the minimum age was 12, and the half-time system was abolished in 1920.

54. Although the 1847 Ten Hours Act did not apply to men, they were effectively included as it was impossible to run a mill on male labour alone. Women have traditionally formed a high proportion of the cotton trade's employees. In 1901 they accounted for 62% of the town's textile workforce. It was often alleged that they were more amenable to the harsh, unremitting discipline of factory work than men. There was probably some truth in this but the main reason was that they earned, on average, only a half to two-thirds of the wages of their male counterparts. Note the women's hair safely piled high on the head, and the tradition of decorating the weaving shed on special occasions.

55. Pictures like these should invoke many memories: the tap on the window from the 'knocker up', or the mills' quaint nicknames – 'Lather Box', 'Mushroom', 'Owd Gant's' and 'Pinch Noggin'. In the noisy, cramped weaving sheds with their whitewashed walls, narrow 'weavers' alleys' and gas-lighting the clog-shod employees communicated by lipreading. Weavers were fined for all faults, 'floats', so they pulled back the cloth unless they were adept at 'dressing the float' – invisible mending. Their work was supervised by over-lookers, 'tacklers'. In 1913 weavers' wages averaged 26/4 per week assuming they worked four looms. These wages would be 'tipped up' to mother as she provided all their necessities.

56. Blackburn figured prominently in the development of the power loom. William Dickinson's 'Blackburn loom' of 1828 introduced picking sticks to propel the shuttle. The inventors John Osbaldeston, James Bullough and William Kenworthy were all employed in Hornby's Brookhouse Mills. Joseph Harrison's and William Dickinson's looms were acclaimed and used for eighty years or more. In 1894 James Northrop patented his automatic loom. The weft was replenished from a rotating hopper or 'battery' which automatically refilled the empty shuttle. These looms were manufactured at Henry Livesey's Greenbank works from 1902. An early, belt driven, example is illustrated. Despite their potential, allowing one weaver to operate twenty-four rather than four looms, they were only slowly accepted. As opportunities for productive reinvestment and rationalisation were missed, King Cotton's crown slipped.

In the Factory   Out of the Factory

OH, WHAT A DIFFERENCE!

57. Despite the gloomy forebodings of their opponents, the Factory Acts did not ruin the textile industry. Their provisions included prohibiting children from cleaning and oiling machinery in motion and made regulations governing the use of steam to make the sheds more humid. Hand-threaded shuttles were not made compulsory until the 1950's, so the unhygienic practice of 'kissing the shuttle', to suck the thread of a new cop through the eye, continued. By 1875 the hours of work were generally 6 a.m. to 5.30 p.m. daily and 6 a.m. to 1 p.m. on Saturday, a 56½ hour week. From 1902 mills closed at Saturday noon but Saturday working continued until 1946. With more leisure time to enjoy, the sharp contrast between noisy mills and tranquil countryside is reflected in this postcard.

ENTRANCE. QUEENS PARK BLACKBURN.

58. *Entrance, Queen's Park circa 1935.* Queen's Park, formerly Audley Recreation Ground, received its present name on 20th June 1887 when it was dedicated as a Golden Jubilee memorial to Queen Victoria. Although her popularity had waned during her indulgently long years of seclusion following the death of Prince Albert in 1861, Queen Victoria was esteemed as never before in the latter years of her reign. A crowd of over 20,000 people witnessed the inauguration ceremony of the thirty-three acre park; and it was reported that from this entrance one could see as far as Pendle Hill and Longridge Fell – how times have changed! Note the telephone box in the foreground and the outbuildings of Queen's Park Hospital, formerly the Union Workhouse, on the hill behind.

Bowling Green, Queen's Park, Blackburn

59. *Bowling Green, Queen's Park circa 1910.* In the nineteenth century drink was the chief leisure pursuit of the working classes. The pub was the social centre and drunkenness a major problem. As working conditions improved and people found themselves with more spare time, so the middle classes became increasingly concerned about how that time should be spent. There followed the organisation and codification of many sports including football, cricket — and bowls, a long established popular sport. The Blackburn Subscription Bowling Club existed in 1731, though it was forced to move from its original green at Cicely Hole with the coming of the railway. The link with pubs continued as many of the newer ones were built with a bowling green adjacent. Later, greens were provided in the public parks.

60. *Corporation Park Gates 1907.* The fifty acre site of the Corporation Park was purchased by the Corporation from the lord of the manor, Joseph Feilden, in January 1855. As a condition the Corporation was required to construct roads on the East and West sides of the park. The natural advantages of the site were skilfully enhanced by planting shrubberies and groves of young trees; and by the construction of ornamental walks, fountains and picturesque lakes. The work, under the direction of Messrs. Henderson and McGregor, proceeded rapidly. The total cost was over £14,700, a third of which came from the sale of part of the Town Moor to the various railway companies. Notice how small are the trees on each side of the main arch, which is surmounted by the Borough Arms.

THE FOUNTAIN
CORPORATION PARK
BLACKBURN. 47

61. *The Fountain, Corporation Park 1907.* A tablet on the entrance records that 'This park was publicly opened on the 22nd day of October 1857, during the mayoralty of William Pilkington Esq., by whose munificence the four ornamental fountains were presented to the Borough'. The proceedings were watched by most of the town's population and several thousand visitors. According to the London 'Illustrated Times': *Of course a procession was called into requisition which entered the park amid salvos of artillery which contributed to do honour to the occasion and to alarm most of the ladies present.* The Mayor's Opening Declaration was followed by a *flourish of trumpets and another roar of guns* which interfered with the subsequent speeches.

Corporation Park, Blackburn

72052

62. *Corporation Park circa 1910.* Again in 1857 it was written that *the valley through which the Blakewater's sluggish murky stream is forced has everyday become more resonant with the busy hum of human industry; tall chimneys have risen on every hand. The thickly set houses are overflowing with a teeming population of our fellow creatures. Until now there has been no place of public resort provided... to which the overwrought artisan could repair, on the cessation of his daily toil; where he could please the eye and invigorate the body, and for a while forget the strife, din and trouble of human existence.* Previously people *were in the habit of walking up Preston New Road for recreation and enjoyment.* This Edwardian group seems quite content to be picnicking amongst the unmown grass.

63. *'The Cannons' circa 1905.* Two Russian cannons captured at Sebastopol were presented to the Borough by Lord Panmure, Secretary of War, as a reminder of the British victories in the Crimean War. They were placed on bastions overlooking the town at the summit of the Corporation Park and were fired during the opening ceremony. A carriage drive was constructed to the battery by unemployed operatives during the Cotton Famine in 1863-64. The wooden carriages slowly rotted and the cannons disappeared in the salvage drive for World War 2. Alongside the cannons for many years stood several German field guns, prizes of World War 1. These had been sold for scrap in 1937 together with the rusting World War 1 tank in Queen's Park.

64. *Opening of the Bandstand, Corporation Park 1909.* On September 17th, 1909 over 6,000 people assembled in the Corporation Park for the formal opening of the new bandstand by Councillor J.H. Higginson. The octagonal bandstand, constructed of ornamental ironwork, was regarded as one of the most up-to-date in the country. It was encircled by terraces and enclosed by iron railings wherein for a penny 1,200 people could be seated on collapsible iron chairs. The opening performance was given by the band of the Border Regiment; the works played included a selection from Lehar's 'The Merry Widow' and some of Harry Lauder's songs.

65. *Corporation Park circa 1930.* In the distance are rows of tightly packed houses amongst mill chimneys belching smoke which almost obliterates the view; a panorama familiar to an older generation. The sky cleared only during the Wakes week shutdown, or — more ominously — during stoppages or strikes. In the foreground the bandstand and ornamental lakes are prominent in their sylvan setting; the contrast could not be greater. The lakes, originally known as 'the Can' and 'the Big Can', were part of Pemberton Clough Waterworks, the town's original water supply. The water was conveyed in wooden pipes to standpipes on various street corners where daily it was sold by the bucketful until the water mains were laid in 1847.

COPY NOOK — BLACKBURN

66. *Copy Nook circa 1905.* Gillies map of 1822 shows two long rows of cottages, surrounded by fields, at 'Far Coppy Nook'. A footpath (now Audley Lane) led to Audley Hall, once a Benedictine nunnery; it was demolished in June 1888. Development of the Audley estate began around 1846 when Henry Shaw, the brewer, built Audley House and the adjoining Malt Kilns off Turkey Row (Audley Street). Close by, on Dock Street, was the town's only windmill. Within forty years the Higher Audley district had been developed. This view shows the once familiar Copy Nook Police Station and, to the left, William Culshaw's saddler's shop. Originally a handloom weaver's cottage, the groundfloor loom-shop's triple windows are still evident. All the buildings have now vanished.

67. *Frederick Row circa 1905.* In 1822 there were few houses between Knuzden and Bottomgate. At Furthergate the branch road to Accrington joined the Blackburn, Addingham, and Cocking End turnpike to Burnley. Close by this junction in 1835 Rodgett and Brierley built a spinning mill and shortly afterwards a weaving shed. Furthergate Mill was damaged during the 'Plug-drawing' riots of 1842, being the first target of the rioters approaching from Accrington. Frederick Row, then fronting open fields, was probably built to house workers from the mill. It was a memorable day when the children had their photograph taken. By 1905 the row had been engulfed by new houses. The mill and the cottages have been demolished but the row's name lives on.

68. *Whalley Range 1905.* In 1845 a track left James Street, by St. John's Church, and ran through the fields past the house called Brookhouse, meeting the Blakewater just beyond Brookhouse Mills. Sixty years later Swallow Street Mill occupied the site of Brookhouse and the track had become Whalley Range. Beyond Cowper Street, right, is Balfour Lund's hairdresser's and photographer's shop. On the left, at the corner of Troy Street, is Whalley Range Council School. Originally a Presbyterian school, it closed when Bangor Street School opened in January 1912. Eventually the building became better known as The People's College but later was demolished. In 1946 the adjacent disused church on Troy Street was converted into the Community Theatre; it closed in 1978.

BASTWELL, BLACKBURN

271.A.

69. *Whalley New Road, Bastwell circa 1915.* The name Bastwell has an intriguing origin. In the thirteenth century it was spelt Baddestwysel, which in Old English refers to a person called 'Badd' who settled by a fork in the river, 'twisla'. William Kenworthy, of the cotton firm Hornby and Kenworthy, erected a handsome house, Brookhouse Lodge, standing in spacious grounds a little south of Bastwell Bridge. The house was purchased in 1859 by the Sisters of Notre Dame and was converted into a college for young ladies. The view has changed little since Mrs. Ibbotson served Henry Shaw's ales and stout at the Bastwell Hotel. Now the Post Office, the shop on the right was for many years occupied by John Fowler − boot, shoe and clog maker.

70. *Little Harwood War Memorial 1923.* The Little
Harwood War Memorial was erected by public subscription in honour of the men of Little Harwood who
made the supreme sacrifice in the Great War. The imposing tower, eight feet square and thirty-three feet
high, containing a four dial clock, was built in Darley
Dale brown stone by ex-servicemen. On August 11th,
1923 over 12,000 people watched the memorial being
unveiled by Major General A. Solly-Flood.

71. *Bowling Green, St. Stephen's Club 1923.* This photograph, taken after the unveiling ceremony, shows from the left: Major General Solly-Flood, Quartermaster Sergeant William Grimbaldeston V.C., the Mayor (James Ramsay) and the Mayoress, Private James Pitts V.C. and Colonel Birtwistle. These were the first two Blackburn soldiers to be awarded the Victoria Cross. Private Pitts won his medal during the Boer War for holding his position for fifteen hours whilst under heavy fire from an enemy who were only sixteen yards away. Sergeant Grimbaldeston won his medal in 1917 for single handedly capturing a German blockhouse which was preventing the British advance.

72. *Little Harwood Club 1905.* Little Harwood Hall was for over four hundred years the ancestral home of the Claytons. When the Hall was sold by Colonel Clayton in 1815, it was still surrounded by fields; there were extensive gardens, and several spacious hot houses containing vines, peach and apricot trees. A valuable rookery, which later became a popular place for picnics, was also attached to the property. Whilst most of the building had retained the characteristic low seventeenth century mullion windows, the north front had been rebuilt in brick around 1730. The Hall was opened as the headquarters of St. Stephen's Conservative Club by Sir Harry Hornby M.P. on 21st April 1894; so it has remained — but long since lost its rural setting.

73. *Beech Tree Inn, Cob Wall circa 1907*. James Bradley stands outside the beerhouse shortly after he took over the tenancy. Dutton's Salford Brewery was founded by Thomas Dutton and his son William in 1799. They soon realised the potential of the tied-house system. Their first purchase was the Golden Ball on Blakey Moor, followed by the Hare and Hounds at Lammack, the George and Dragon on Northgate and the Lord Nelson at Salford. Only the Hare and Hounds remains. All family ties were relinquished in 1897 and the company joined the Whitbread Group in 1964. Many will recall their strong ale, Old Ben, bottled under the name 'Oh Be Joyful' or, more commonly, 'OBJ'. The Beech Tree still stands, little altered.

74. *Swan Brewery, Larkhill Street 1928.* The liveried draymen of the Blackburn Brewery Company pose proudly alongside their Leyland wagons. They are, from the left: Jimmy Preston, 'Jock' McKnight, George Hall and Arthur Howitt. The emblem of Mr. Harry Bottomley's Swan Brewery, a brass swan, can be seen on each radiator. The wagon on the left has just been refurbished; the oil sidelights remain but the acetylene headlights have been replaced by electric lights. Solid tyres and cobbled streets must have ensured that the beer arrived well and truly shaken! Shortly afterwards the brewery was taken over by its rival, Duttons. The site of the brewery is now occupied by the Larkhill Health Centre.

75. *New Fire Station, Byrom Street 1921.* Blackburn's first fire station was in Engine Street off Northgate. In 1867 the station was removed to Clayton Street which remained the headquarters of the brigade until the move to Byrom Street. The engines were manned by volunteers until 1882 when a new brigade was formed from members of the Police force. It remained under the control of the Chief Constable until the inception of the National Fire Service in 1941. The photograph shows the vehicles arriving at the new fire station on 8th December 1921. The Byrom Street premises also initially housed the Borough ambulances (one can be seen on the right) and provided stabling for the Mounted Police horses.

76. *Motor Cavalcade 1902.* Lined up outside the Town Hall are members of the Blackburn-based Lancashire Automobile Club prior to their first-ever rally to Clitheroe. Of fourteen starters, only ten managed to complete the journey. None of the cars displays a number plate; these were introduced the following year. On the extreme right is a Sunbeam Mabley — a car which had a strange diamond layout of its wheels and was much prone to capsizing — owned by Mr. Fred Hodgkinson of Higher Feniscowles Hall. Standing on the steps with her father Richard Lord — whose car, a Southport-made Vulcan, had broken down — was a two-year old girl who was later to be the wife of Alderman Robert Mottershead.

77. *Daisyfield Industrious Bees Co-operative Society's store, Knuzden circa 1910.* In 1868 there were seven Co-operative Societies in Blackburn. Mergers followed, until in 1920 the remaining societies – Grimshaw Park, Blackburn Industrial, and Daisyfield – united to form the Blackburn (Amalgamated) Co-operative Society Limited. Despite the depression that followed, the society prospered under the direction of General Manager George Whiteside, soon having over sixty branches and a fine new Emporium on Town Hall Street. The 'Co-op' moved to its new store in the shopping precinct late in 1971 and the Emporium re-opened in October 1975 as the town's Central Library. The Knuzden shop is now a garden-fronted house. Knuzden Brook (behind) marks the Borough's eastern boundary, and flows on to form the Blakewater.

78. *J.J. Simpson, Grocer and Butcher, Bank Top circa 1904.* As competition became keener shopkeepers adorned their windows in an attempt to attract customers. As the 'Practical Grocer' reminded the trade: 'A regular succession of attractive windows, of original and striking designs, will grow to be a subject of interest and remark with the public, an interest which the utmost should be done to sustain.' Here John Simpson, with his sons and assistants, poses proudly in the doorway. The side window advertises his 'Eiffel Tower Specialities'. The poster shows us what housewives had to pay for their provisions, including 'splendid breakfast bacon' at 7d. per lb., and tea varying from 1/4 to 2/- per lb. The shop, with its distinctive upper window, can still be found at the corner of Stansfeld Street.

79. *Ainsworth's Hardware Shop, Bolton Road, Ewood circa 1925.* The prices on Ainsworth's wares make interesting reading. The spades range from 1/11 to 6/6, whilst for 2/- you could buy a watering can, or a saw for 3/9. The window is packed with many other indispensible household items. Note the lampshades and the variety of wicker baskets. Some familiar names also appear including Gillette razors, Cherry Blossom boot polish, and Mansion polish. On the right is Ewood Mill: originally a water-driven carding mill, it was enlarged over the years and rebuilt following a fire in 1888. The mill, in 1925 operated by James Livesey, later became part of the Birtwistle Group, and is now occupied by Redmayne and Isherwood.

80. *James Cort, Fish, Fruit and Rabbit Salesman 1913.* Shopping weeks were introduced early this century with the intention of making Blackburn the 'natural Shopping Centre of North East Lancashire'. According to the Northern Daily Telegraph on 24th October 1913 *The tradesmen's turnout competitions, the most popular feature so far as the public are concerned, were judged on the Market Square yesterday afternoon, in the presence of several thousand spectators.* Special prizes were presented by the Blackburn Wholesale Fruiterers. First prize in the four-wheeled vehicle section went to James Cort of Copy Nook. The Shopping Week was apparently a great success. The decorated and illuminated trams, the shop window displays and the usual market attracted an enormous crowd into town on the Saturday.

81. *Tattersall's delivery van circa 1910*. William Tattersall's chain-driven, three-wheeled delivery van was based on a popular Raleigh motor-tricycle chassis of the period. After buying out his partner in 1878, his wholesale provision merchant's business prospered and when he died in 1929, it ranked as one of the largest in the North of England. William Tattersall – a staunch Liberal, Justice of the Peace, and Mayor in 1900 – is perhaps best remembered for his active association with Wesleyan Methodism. He was the doyen of local preachers, being placed on the Plan in 1864 and for over half a century was connected with Clayton Street Church and Sunday School. His obituary in the Blackburn Times rightly described him as Blackburn's 'Grand Old Man of Methodism'.

82. *Mrs. Lewis 1905*. Mrs. Elizabeth Lewis, 'The Drunkard's Friend', is easily identified by her distinctive, but by now unfashionable, hairstyle of long ringlets. She was well known for her Lees Hall Temperance Mission. The hall, which was built over her husband's coachworks in St. Peter Street, was named after Dr. F.R. Lees of Leeds (a prominent temperance advocate) and opened by him on June 18th, 1891. Despite failing health in later years, she never wearied of calling on the people to 'Sign the Pledge' and give up intoxicating drink. When she died in 1924 she was mourned by countless thousands throughout the world.

83. *Football Association Cup Winners 1891.* In this era the Rovers were redoubtable cup-fighters. They had won the F.A. Cup in 1884, 1885, 1886 and 1890. In 1891 they again swept every team before them and in the final, at Kennington Oval, they beat Notts County 3-1 with goals by Dewar, Southworth and Townley. A tremendous reception awaited the players on their return. They were cheered from the train and driven around the town in a wagonette, preceded by the Blackburn Borough Band. Blackburn Rovers F.C., founded 1875, originally played on a rented field off Preston New Road which had a pond in the middle. Rather than fill it in, it was roofed over with planks and camouflaged with sods. The Rovers then moved to Alexandra Meadows and Leamington Road before arriving at Ewood in 1890.

84. *Strong Dick: Bottle and Bowl Trick.* Richard Thompson was better known to an earlier generation as 'Strong Dick', a professional weightlifter and itinerant entertainer. He gave weekly exhibitions of weightlifting on Blackburn Market Place, supplementing this by wriggling through hoops of varying sizes. He was a man of many parts: onetime evangelist, he danced with the Floradora girls and in 1928 walked to London to see the Rovers win the F.A. Cup. Less successful was his well-publicised attempt to walk around the world; the story goes that he walked as far as Macclesfield, where he turned back because a local farmer was unable to show him the way to China.

85. *'Owd Chipper'* — real name Robert Reynolds — was a well known character at the turn of the century, and was 88 when he died in 1912. As a boy he acquired the nickname 'Chipper'. In his thirties he abandoned employment as a spinner, and constructed a truck with a kennel-like top; and inside this he created a peep-show of toy soldiers depicting one of Wellington's battles. Children would bring old rags to him for a peep. When asked which was Wellington, his reply would be 'Ony on 'em' and so 'Ony on 'em, Chipper' came into the Blackburn vernacular. It is claimed that over 6,000 postcards of him were issued. Fame indeed!

86. *Hornby Statue 1912.* William Henry Hornby was in 1851 the town's first Mayor. In the political arena he earned both the grudging admiration of his opponents and his nickname 'Th' owd Gam' Cock'. The statue, which originally stood in Limbrick overlooking Sudell Cross, was the gift of John Margerison, who for over fifty years was employed in Hornby's Brookhouse mills. The striking bronze sculpture, by Mr. Bruce Joy, was unveiled on 18th July 1912 by Sir 'Harry' Hornby, his eldest son. With his distinctive monocle and side whiskers, Sir Harry was a familiar and well-loved figure in Blackburn streets for half a century until he died in 1928. The statue, albeit without its ornate plinth, now stands alongside the Town Hall.

87. *Gladstone Statue circa 1910.* The statue of the Right Honourable William Ewart Gladstone was erected on the Boulevard in November 1899 and unveiled by the Earl of Aberdeen. The ten foot high statue of white Italian marble, was sculpted by Mr. J. Adams-Acton and stands on a pedestal of red Petershead granite. Four times Prime Minister, Gladstone's ability is best summed up in Lord Salisbury's striking tribute, 'the most brilliant intellect that has been placed at the service of the State since Parliamentary Government began'. In September 1955 the statue was resited outside the old Technical College; it has recently been uprooted again and can now be found on Northgate facing the Public Halls — it, too, deprived of its ornamental surround.

PALACE THEATRE, BLACKBURN.

88. *Palace Theatre 1905.* When the New Palace Theatre opened in December 1899, it had the largest gallery in Lancashire. For many years it was the premier variety theatre of the McNaghten Vaudeville Circuit. Increasing competition from the radio and talking pictures, combined with a slump in the cotton trade, resulted in its closure in 1932, though four years later it reopened as a cinema. On the left is Jubilee Street, named after the Jubilee brewery erected in 1809, King George III's Jubilee year. The brewery was replaced in 1820 by Bannister Eccles' ill-fated Jubilee Mill – the 'Dandy' mill as it was nick-named after the new daintier looms introduced there. The mill was destroyed by fire in 1842, but its memory survives in Dandy Walk.

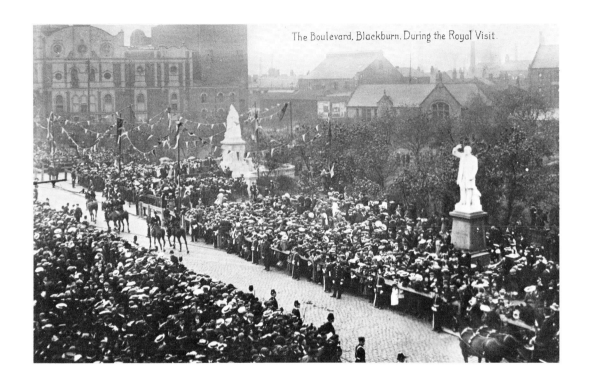

The Boulevard, Blackburn, During the Royal Visit.

89. *The Boulevard, Saturday, 30th September 1905.* An estimated crowd of 200,000 people, brought by special trains and trams, lined the route from Billinge End to the Boulevard for the visit of H.R.H. Princess Louise. The Princess had come to unveil a statue of her mother, Queen Victoria, which had been erected on the Boulevard by public subscription following the Queen's death on 22nd January 1901. The eleven-foot high statue of white Sicilian marble on a light grey granite plinth shows the crowned and robed figure of Queen Victoria holding an orb and sceptre. The sculptor was Mr. Bertram Mackennal and the statue was a replica of one he had erected in Ballarat, Australia.

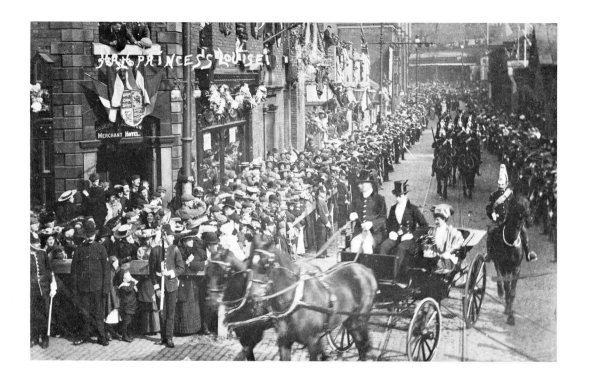

90. H.R.H. Princess Louise and her husband His Grace the Duke of Argyll had stayed overnight at Wycollar as guests of Sir William and Lady Coddington. They were greeted by the Mayor at Billinge End and then continued to the Boulevard by way of the Town Hall. On arrival the Princess advanced to the centre of the dais and gave the tassled silk cord a pull. Then according to one newspaper report 'amid cheers in the full glory of the noonday sun was revealed to the expectant multitude the dignified figure of Queen Victoria.' After the speeches the procession returned to the Town Hall for luncheon. Princess Louise is seen leaving Jubilee Street with her escort from the Duke of Lancaster's Own Imperial Yeomanry.

91. The inhabitants occupying premises on or just off the line of the procession responded cheerfully to the reception committee's appeal to decorate their premises. As a large crowd was expected barriers were erected along the route. Mills, offices and banks closed for the day and shops suspended business from 10.00 a.m. to 3.00 p.m. This was, after all, only the second Royal Visit to the town. The proceedings over, the Guard of Honour also left the Boulevard by way of Jubilee Street. On the left is the partially completed new façade of the Princes Theatre, now the site of the Telephone Exchange. Opposite are some of the buildings of the old Corporation Electricity Works, which too have been demolished.

Visit of Princess Louise to Blackburn. Sept. 30th, 1905.—No. 23.

92. The Guard of Honour was mounted along various portions of the route by the Blackburn batteries of the 1st. Volunteer Battalion East Lancashire Regiment and the 3rd. Lancashire Royal Garrison Artillery (Volunteers). Both military units had their own magnificent bands. The 3rd. L.R.G.A. (Vols.) are seen outside the Town Hall. On the right, in front of the District Bank, stand youngsters from the detachment of the Church Lads' Brigade who were stationed from Exchange Street along King William Street. Here, as elsewhere, the spectators have occupied every vantage point. The District Bank, after rebuilding, became the Westminster Bank; Williams and Glyn's bank now occupies the corner site opposite.

93. At night the streets were thronged. The two camera clubs attracted large crowds to displays on the front of their respective premises, at Sudell Cross and Church Street, of lantern views of that morning's pageant. Portraits of the Mayor, Borough Council Members, Members of the Royal Family and landscape pictures were also shown. In Corporation Park the Blackburn Town Prize Band gave a promenade concert. In Queen's Park, which was illuminated with oriental lanterns, a military band performed selections of music. This was followed by a grand firework display. On Sunday the Princess visited Sir James and Lady de Hoghton at Hoghton Tower, before leaving for Inverary early on Monday morning.

94. *Preston New Road, 2.00 p.m. Thursday 10th July 1913.* This was the crowd returning to the Town Hall, hoping for a second glimpse of King George V and Queen Mary. Their Majesties were visiting the town and had driven through the Witton and Corporation Parks before going on to Roe Lee Mills. From there they would return to the Town Hall. His Majesty had come to lay the foundation stone of the New Public Halls in Northgate. This he would accomplish from a dais in front of the Town Hall; a tall order one may think, but not impossible in that modern age!

95. This is how the proceedings were described in the official programme: *The presentations having been made, the Mayor will hand to His Majesty an ELECTRIC SWITCH. His Majesty will then, by pressing the switch, lay the foundation stone of the New Public Halls in Northgate. When the stone is laid a flag will be unfurled by means of electricity, on the flagstaff of the Exchange Hall, in view of the assembled multitude.* The task completed, the photograph shows their Majesties about to leave for Darwen in their Rolls Royce, which is flying the Royal Standard. That evening 50,000 people watched a 'grand military torchlight tattoo' in Witton Park.

St. Alban's Field Day.

96. *St. Alban's Field Day circa 1910.* This well dressed procession is seen crossing the Blakewater in Brookhouse Lane. St. Alban's R.C. Church, the Mother Church of Blackburn's Catholic community, has an interesting history. The first church was erected in Old Chapel Street in 1773 and was rebuilt seven years later. The third building, erected on the present site in St. Alban's Place in 1824, was demolished in 1898. The foundation stone of the 'new' church was laid on 15th October 1898 and the church opened on 8th December 1901. Brookhouse Mill is in the centre background, but the houses beyond have gone. Swallow Street Mill on the right, has now been replaced by a modern housing estate.

97. *St. Paul's Procession circa 1910.* St. Paul's Church, built by subscription, was first opened as a Chapel of Ease in 1791 and consecrated in 1829. It was the second oldest church in the Borough and reputedly the most ugly with few redeeming features. The banner, that of St. Paul's Sunday and Day Schools, has the school buildings depicted on it. The procession, passing along West Park Road, is approaching Dukes Brow. Behind the banner can be seen the roof of the conservatory in Corporation Park. The wall of Alexandra Meadows is on the right; later the bowling club-house would be built here. In more committed times taking part in such a procession of witness to one's faith was a highlight of many lives.

98. *Church of the Saviour Procession, Mosley Street circa 1910.* Processions, whether they were Whit walks, or to celebrate May Day or local Field Days, usually had a religious basis, and gave pleasure to participants and onlookers alike. The Church of the Saviour, founded in 1901 in open fields at Longshaw, became a separate parish in 1923, and is now surrounded by a council housing estate. The procession has reached the junction with Alaska Street. Note the variety of dress displayed. The Harrison Arms, left, and the adjoining shop have been demolished, although the houses beyond remain. Christ Church School in the background is no longer a school; and the church spire and Crossfield Mill's sturdy tower have disappeared.

THE AMBULANCE REVIEW BLACKBURN (6)

99. *The Ambulance Review, Ewood Park 23rd July 1906.* In the late 1880's the Royal Infirmary acquired a 'horse ambulance van' which was housed at the Old Bull Stables in St. Peter Street. According to a contemporary report, its value 'in alleviating the suffering of those being conveyed, maimed, and in great pain, from the place of accident to the Infirmary' was inestimable. In 1903 the Borough Police acquired a new, more modern, version. The Blackburn Corps of the St. John's Ambulance Brigade was formed in 1900 and the women's section was registered two years later. One of their busiest nights came in April 1928 when the Rovers brought home the F.A. Cup. Following the move from Princes Street, the Brigade's headquarters is now at Lees Hall.

100. *Cuckoo Hall circa 1907.* In 1848 Cuckoo Hall stood alone midway between the Jolly Dragoon Inn at Four Lane Ends and the Hare and Hounds. Despite its quaint name it was simply a row of four cottages, seen here before the fields beyond Lammack Road were built on. Interestingly a previous innkeeper of the 'Jolly Dragoon' had been John Osbaldeston, the inventor, who later regretted the money he sank in 'that Tom and Jerry shop'. Nearby, in June 1879, a Bronze Age burial urn, evidence of early settlers, was unearthed by workmen engaged on the site of the water tank, now used as a viewpoint. The last residents moved out in 1968, the cottages being demolished shortly afterwards. Only the cobbled track and the overgrown walled gardens remain.

101. *Roman Road, Blackamoor circa 1905.* The straight line of the Roman road from Manchester to Ribchester bisected the Parish of Blackburn. Though no trace remains within the town, the road came over Blacksnape, through Blackamoor and Grimshaw Park, and crossed the Blakewater near Salford. It would have passed behind St. John's Church before climbing up to Four Lane Ends and on to Ramsgreave. The road surface eighty years ago appears to be little better than it probably was in Roman times. Fortunately today the road has been improved. The lamp-post and letter box have gone but the cottages remain, now reroofed and modernised.

102. *Lower Darwen 1907.* The name has changed over the centuries. In Norman times 'Nether Derwent' was an appurtenance of the feudal estate of Walton-le-Dale. In 1523 the township was referred to, somewhat unflatteringly, as 'Derwent Inferior' and by 1565 a third variation 'Nether Darwyne' appears. The population in 1801 was 1646, which more than doubled in seventy years with the coming of the cotton factories. In 1879 part of Lower Darwen was included in the Borough of Blackburn; the remainder followed in 1974. Here we see the Congregational Church, left; Lower Darwen Mills, centre right; and the Railway Station beyond with, to its left, the United Methodists' Sunday School – both now demolished. Note the absence of later modern housing developments.

103. *Lower Darwen Station circa 1905.* The railway came to Lower Darwen in 1847. The only station building in the early years would have been a wooden shed covered by a wagon sheet. This structure was on one occasion stolen and later found two miles away at Eccleshill, being used as a hencote. Part of the fabric of the substantial buildings shown in the photograph was believed to have come from the demolished Great Bolton Street station, the headquarters of the former Bolton, Blackburn, Clitheroe and West Yorkshire Railway. The station closed in 1958 and now only the two footbridge pillars remain following demolition of the buildings in 1964.

104. *Old Mill, Lower Darwen circa 1885.* The mill was built about 1774 by Thomas Eccles, who lived in Lower Darwen House which can be seen on the right. It was a four storey water-driven spinning mill which would have contained Hargreaves 'spinning jennies', Arkwright water twist frames, and later Crompton spinning mules. When steam engines became a commercial proposition and began to supersede the water wheel, the Old Mill was one of the first to introduce them. The turret on the roof housed the factory bell which was used to call the people to work. The workmen are demolishing the mill and the adjacent house to make room for the new weaving sheds.

105. *Sandy Lane, Lower Darwen circa 1904.* The Eccles family was one of the earliest employers to adopt an enlightened policy towards the educational needs of the children in its mills. The Lower Darwen Factory School dated from 1817, and there the children were taught the 'three R's'. 'Half Timers' attended school in the morning and worked in the mill in the afternoon. The foundation stone of the school shown above was laid on 13th June 1896 by Mrs. Richard Eccles, and this school was opened six months later by Sir John Brunner. The photograph was taken before Kingston Place was built and the wall on the right demolished when the road was widened.

106. *Canal Street, Mill Hill circa 1910.* The Leeds and Liverpool Canal, completed in 1816, had taken forty-plus years to build. Had Longbottom's original plans been adhered to it would have bypassed Blackburn and followed the Ribble and Calder Valleys. Despite increasing railway competition, the short boats carried materials and finished products to and from the town for almost one hundred and fifty years. The last commercial traffic (coal from Bank Hall Colliery, Burnley, to Whitebirk power station) finally succumbed in the big freeze of 1963. The Navigation Inn, on the right, remains today but the Angela Street shop is now a house. The present-day towpath wall does not exist, and Bower House Fold Bridge on Shorrock Lane is the original. Notice also the important telephone route following the towpath.

MILL HILL Rly STATION.

107. *Mill Hill Station circa 1910.* When the Blackburn to Preston railway opened in 1846, Mill Hill consisted of four isolated hamlets — Overlockshaw, Bower House Fold, Stakes Hall and Mill Hill. Stakes Hall, long since demolished, was for nearly three hundred years the home of the Astley family. The Turners bought the Stakes Hall estate and built their calico printing works there. In 1843 the print works and estate were sold to Joseph Eccles of Mill Hill House, who demolished the old print shops and erected the Mill Hill Mill. As the area developed a station was required and this opened in 1884. Sadly, the fine canopy has been demolished and the railway sidings have gone; the Waterfall Mill, behind, remains.

108. *New Chapel Street 1913*. In 1847 this street was merely a track running beside a tram road which linked Mill Hill Mill with the canal. That year Joseph Eccles erected the original Congregational Chapel and school, right, which gave the street its name. The congregation soon outgrew the first floor Chapel; thus Mill Hill Congregational Church, in the distance, opened in September 1860. In 1912-13 its exterior was renovated and the tower re-erected; regrettably the church has now been demolished. To the left is Pioneer Mill's chimney, the first mill to be built in the twentieth century. Flags are flying over Ingham's pawnbroker's shop and the signs on the gable of Tipping's fried fish shop are just discernible today.

109. *New Chapel Street 1912.* This view, from the opposite direction to the last, shows (on the left) the buildings of Overlockshaw which then housed a blacksmith and grocery store. On the right, adjoining Kenyon's 'cheap drapery establishment', were a fruiterer and a newsagent. Beyond these were to be found a confectioner, grocer, tripe dealer, hosier and bootmaker. In the distance signs can be seen painted on Lawson's butcher's shop. Beside this, behind the boards, was the large mill lodge which fed Mill Hill Mill. This was filled in, and in May 1936 Mill Hill Gardens were formally opened. Beyond the lodge was the Mill Hill Brick and Tile Works which supplied building materials for the district as it developed.

110. *Mill Hill Bridge Street circa 1910.* Although the bridge appears quite new, Mill Hill Bridge was the original crossing point over the River Darwen linking the otherwise isolated community with Blackburn. In 1848 the road forked left to Witton Stocks and right to Griffin. Before reaching the Griffin's Head the road passed through an extensive brickfield. These bricks would have supplied the developing Witton, Griffin, Redlam and, possibly, Mill Hill areas. On the left is the Victorian façade of the Mill Hill Hotel, built in 1902, with a large bowling green to the rear. Beyond are the houses of Merlyn Terrace, now part of Nares Road. In the distance only the chimney of Witton Bank is visible behind the trees.

111. *Griffin circa 1910*. At the end of the eighteenth century the old Preston and Blackburn road was diverted, widened and re-bridged under the provisions of the Blackburn and Walton Cop Trust. The 1848 Ordnance Survey map shows the Griffin's Head with, at the foot of Redlam Brow, the 'Griffin Gate' tollbar. Sixty years later the area had been developed. On the right, surmounted by its sign, stood the Boundary Arms, so called as the Parliamentary boundary crossed the road here. The shops on the right, which have now been demolished, included a chemist, fish dealer, newsagent, pork butcher and a boot maker. The ornate lamp and horse trough in front of the Griffin Inn have also disappeared.

112. *Cherry Tree 1903*. In the eighteenth century Cherry Tree House was the home of the Boardman family. Prominent nonconformists, they were among the original trustees of the Old Independent Chapel at Tockholes. This view of the tram terminus, with Green Lane on the right, shows how rural Cherry Tree was eighty years ago. The tramway was extended from Witton Stocks to Cherry Tree in October 1903. Despite its 1902 datestone, only half of Fairfield Terrace had been built. The last tram ran on 31st March 1939. The outbreak of war, and the ensuing shortage of fuel oil and spare parts for the buses, made the Tramways Committee seriously consider reopening it, but the cost of refitting the overhead wire was prohibitive.

113. *Roddlesworth Valley, 24th August 1867.* By 1860 coalowners around Wigan felt they needed a rail link with East Lancashire and proposed the formation of a company to construct the line. Fearing loss of its territory, the Lancashire and Yorkshire Railway proposed a link from Cherry Tree, via Chorley, to Wigan. This was authorised by an Act of Parliament in July 1864, and was constructed jointly by the Lancashire and Yorkshire Railway Company and the Lancashire Union Railway Company. It was opened on 1st November 1869. The steep gradients on either side of the summit at Brinscall made the line difficult to work. The line has long been closed and its track lifted, though some features like the embankment and viaduct at Feniscowles remain.

114. *Preston Old Road, Feniscowles 1904.* In 1276 it was spelt Feinycholes; the Old English elements making up the name are 'fenny' = marshy and 'scholes' = huts. Livesey, written as Liveseye in 1227, just as clearly means the ey or island of 'Leof', which here indicates a firm area of land surrounded by marsh. The village was 'en fête' on Saturday afternoon, 20th August 1902, for the stone laying ceremony of the new Methodist Mission (right). The Mission room, established in 1898 by Mr. and Mrs. Jepson, could no longer accommodate the ever increasing band of worshippers and scholars. The vestibuled entrance has now been replaced by one at the side; note also the old police station, a cottage in the left foreground.

Feniscowles Blackburn

115. *Preston Old Road, Feniscowles circa 1910.* The most important ancient road locally was the highway from Preston to Blackburn and Burnley and into West Yorkshire. The present road through Feniscowles has been greatly improved under the provisions of the road trusts. A branch road linking the turnpike roads to Bolton and Preston was constructed through Livesey. In 1798 William Feilden purchased the Feniscowles estate, built Feniscowles New Hall in 1808 and constructed a deer park round it. A generous benefactor, and for fifteen years a member of Parliament for Blackburn, he was made a baronet in 1846. The view has changed little: a garage has been built on the right, and a housing estate on the left. Feniscowles New Hall is now in ruins.

EW BROWN'S
HOP BEERS.

Pleasington

Evans
Publisher
Preston

116. *Pleasington circa 1915.* Records of the ancient lords of Pleasington, the de Plesyngton family, can be traced back to the early thirteenth century. They were followed by the Ainsworths, who lived at Pleasington Old Hall. During the fifteenth century the village was well known for its alum mines, visited later by King James I, which finally closed in 1659. This village street scene shows little change over the years. Brownlow Terrace, right, adjoining the Golf Course, remains though the barn has been demolished. On the left is a sign for the Railway Hotel which dispensed Matthew Brown's beers. Matthew Brown started brewing beer in Preston in 1830. In 1927 the company bought Nuttall's Lion brewery and transferred operations to there.

117. *Pleasington Station circa 1909.* In 1777 'Pleasington Manor and its fine desmesne' were auctioned at the Black Bull, Blackburn, and sold to Richard Butler, of Preston, for £11,000. His son John built Pleasington New Hall in 1805-1807 with stone from their quarries at Butler's Delph. He paid for John Palmer to build the prominent Pleasington Priory in 1818-19; according to Pevsner, an 'astonishing' church, especially considering the then position of Catholicism. Subsequently the home of Sir Harry Hornby, the New Hall was demolished after his death and the grounds became Blackburn's new cemetery. Pleasington Station is seen here sixty years after the line opened. Another building was later added on the eastbound platform; all have been removed, and the station now comprises two vandalised bus shelters.

118. *Yew Tree Inn circa 1912*. Thomas Whipp must have pulled many pints of Thwaites celebrated beers for thirsty customers. Eanam Brewery was erected soon after 1797. Daniel Thwaites (an excise officer) joined the firm, married the daughter of one of the founders and by 1824 had become the sole owner. After his death control passed to his sons, Daniel and John. The latter retired in 1858. Under the management of 'young' Daniel the business flourished. Daniel, like his brother, had been elected to the first town council in 1851 and later became a magistrate and Member of Parliament. When he died in 1878 the business passed to his daughter Mrs. Elma Yerburgh and is still owned by this family. The Yew Tree, however, closed in 1971, though the building still remains.

119. *Shackerley Toll Bar 1890*. The much needed improvements to the road network in this part of Lancashire began in the 1790's when businessmen, needing better roads by which to convey their merchandise, promoted road schemes to Haslingden, Bolton and Burnley. These were followed in 1826 by a new turnpike road to Preston. Revenue to repay the investors – and supposedly to repair the roads – came from construction and letting of toll bars. Along these routes tolls were levied on those using the roads. This photograph of Shackerley toll bar, which stood on Preston New Road just beyond the Yew Tree Inn, was taken the day the tolls were abolished on 1st November 1890.

120. *Mellor Brook 1906.* The old Clitheroe to Preston road followed the high ground from Whalley through York, Ramsgreave and Mellor until 1810 when what is now the A59, past the Oaks Bar Toll house, was opened through to Samlesbury. Thereafter the old road continued to Preston via Walton-le-Dale until Preston New Road was completed. The two turnpike roads were linked by a branch road at Mellor Brook. This view, which has hardly changed, shows the road junction outside the Feilden Arms in less dangerous days. In the distance Mellor can be seen on the hill with the chimney of Elswick Mill on the left and the spire of St. Mary's Church on the right.

A VIEW IN MELLOR BROOK   NO. 715

121. *Mellor Brook 1905.* At the bottom of Mellor Brow stood the Pack Horse Inn where the packmen would have refreshed themselves and their ponies before climbing the hill. As this would have been an uneven track until the end of the last century, the slippery descent was as difficult as the ascent. The Inn closed, but was used by the Home Guard during World War 2 before it and the adjoining farmhouse were destroyed by fire on 28th September 1944. On the right the row of cottages, known locally as 'Jumbo Entry', have changed little over the years.

CHURCH LANE MELLOR.

122. *Church Lane, Mellor 1905.* Handloom weaving thrived in Mellor during the eighteenth century and caused an influx of cottage weavers. After 1830 competition from the power loom saw many younger weavers drafted into the mills in Blackburn. The population of Mellor declined by almost half in forty years. 'Do you recognise the sweet shop?' asked the sender of the card. A question equally appropriate today as the shop is now the Post Office and Village Store. Beyond is the spire of the Parish Church which opened in 1829, and was founded by a Parliamentary Commissioner's grant. Opposite is St. Mary's National School, seen here before it was extended in 1913. Both buildings benefitted from the generosity of Daniel Thwaites, Lord of the Manor, and his daughter Mrs. Elma Yerburgh.

In the photograph, text visible reads: LAYING FOUNDATION STONE RAWSTORNE MEMORIAL BALDERSTONE

123. *Balderstone Church, Whit Monday 1906.* This fashion-conscious crowd had gathered to witness the laying of the foundation stone of the Rawstorne memorial tower. Robert Atherton Rawstorne was appointed the first vicar of St. Leonard's in 1859, a position he held for thirty-eight years. It was due largely to his work and energy that the church prospered, and the community derived much benefit from his generosity. The handsome tower, which replaced the north porch, is a fitting memorial to the work of the Archdeacon and his wife Cecilia. It was designed by Messrs. Paley and Austin of Lancaster, paid for by relatives and parishioners, and formally completed on 18th April 1907.

124. *Ribchester 1904.* The road linking the Roman forts of Mamucium (Manchester) and Bremetenna-cum (Ribchester) passed through Blackburn. Over the years the Ribble has encroached upon the site of the fort and the remains lying only three feet beneath the present ground level have been much disturbed by building. Comparatively little is known of developments in Ribchester after the Romans left though in the fourteenth century the area suffered a double blow: the village was burnt and pillaged by the Scots in 1332, and seventeen years later over one hundred inhabitants were killed by the Black Death. The present White Bull, formerly the 'Court House', apparently dates from 1707. The Tuscan columns, like two in St. Wilfred's Parish Church, are reputed to be of Roman origin.

125. *Ribchester 1906.* Excavations of the Roman fort were undertaken periodically from the late 1880's. Like the photographer, many Blackburnians caught the tram to Wilpshire and then walked to Ribchester. The photograph shows the old Church crofts being converted into the house known as 'Churchgates'. The old schoolhouse is on the right and two people are investigating one of the finds. The bicycle, or velocipede as it was initially called, became enormously popular in the 1890's following the invention of the pneumatic tyre. It was especially appreciated by women, who were excluded from many sports.

126. *De Tabley Arms 1904.* The inn stands on the south bank of the Ribble at an ancient crossing point, just below Ribchester Bridge. Its name was changed from the Bridge Inn when Lord De Tabley became heir to the Talbot estates around 1830. The present bridge, with its three graceful arches, dates from 1774 and the scene has changed little since James Croston a century ago described the 'charming prospect that meets the eye... all was calm, placid and serene'. The tranquillity today is disturbed by the traffic during the daytime and the music from Lydia's nightclub, as the De Tabley has now become, at night.

New Hall, Ribchester.

127. *New Hall 1910.* Nearby New Hall is a good example of the type of house built for the lesser gentry in the mid-seventeenth century. It has a roofline broken with gables, small mullioned windows and a gabled porch. The hall was built by George Talbot, whose initials and the date 1665 are inscribed in the front wall. Another stone contains, within a moulded panel, the sculpture of a talbot (a breed of hound), the crest of the Talbots. George Talbot was made a Governor of Blackburn Grammar School in 1667. The road has now been widened and realigned and the hall has sadly been allowed to fall into disrepair.

A VIEW IN WILPSHIRE.

128. *A View in Wilpshire 1907.* Records of the de Wylipshire family can be traced back to the thirteenth century when one Adam de Wilpshire gave to the monks of Stanlaw 'half an acre and a fall of land in the vill of Wilpshire'. More recently the townships of Wilpshire-cum-Dinckley were named together as forming one township. In the nineteenth century the population was small and mainly agricultural; after 1830 it declined by a third, suggesting again that handloom weavers from the area moved into Blackburn. This tranquil scene on Knowsley Road, Wilpshire Bottoms, has changed little in the intervening years, though the field beyond on the right has now been developed for housing.

129. *Tram Terminus, Wilpshire circa 1910.* The tramway was extended from the Cemetery to Wilpshire in May 1902. The trams originally terminated in the centre of the road though later, as traffic increased, a lay-by and shelter were built on the left. For forty-five years the trams brought people from the town to walk down Knowsley Road, left, into the countryside and on to Ribchester. After many false alarms the route closed with a few Councillors riding on the last tram on the evening of 21st December 1947. The view has altered slightly over the years. The trees, right, have grown-shrouding 'Rockmount' in the distance; whilst those on the left, the wall, and the tram standards have all vanished.

A VIEW IN WILPSH

130. *Whalley New Road 1908*. The ancient road from Blackburn to Whalley proceeded by Cob Wall, past Little Harwood Hall and Bank Hey to join the old Preston to Clitheroe road (now Parsonage Road) near the Bull's Head. This was superseded by a 'direct' turnpike road from Little Harwood via the New Inn – Whalley Old Road; which in turn was replaced by the present road. In 1848 the only buildings here were the Bull's Head and, opposite it, a smithy. Sixty years on, the Bull's Head has been rebuilt and has competition from the Rising Sun; note its hoardings for Nuttall's Ales and Stout. The handcart on the left is advertising 'Borax dry soap'. Although the ornate lamp has gone, this view from the tram terminus has changed little.

131. *Wilpshire Station circa 1910.* The first sod of the Blackburn, Clitheroe and North Western Junction Railway was cut by Lord Ribblesdale on 30th December 1846. Yates' foundry of Blackburn was responsible for the iron castings. After several setbacks, including the collapse of two arches of the Whalley viaduct, the railway opened on 22nd June 1850. The line terminated at Chatburn for thirty years until the extension to Hellifield was opened. Ribchester station, as it was originally called, opened in 1850 and here, sixty years later, the station master and his staff of five proudly pose for the photographer. The station, Wilpshire for Ribchester, closed in 1958. The station buildings remain, but the footbridge and shelter have been demolished.

132. *The Orphanages, Wilpshire 1911.* James Dixon was co-founder of Blackburn Ragged School. One night he found several small boys sleeping out in a warehouse doorway. After succouring the waifs he made inquiries which resulted in his establishing, along with Thomas Hart, ropemaker, a building fund for an orphanage in 1886. After an uphill struggle the first building was opened on 23rd July 1891 by Miss Derbyshire who had purchased the admirable site. This building was enlarged five years later and the second building opened in 1905. For over forty years James Dixon and his wife were to be affectionately known as 'father' and 'mother' to hundreds of orphans. The original orphanage (on the right) has been demolished; only the second 'newer' building survives.

BROWN HILL WHALLEY NEW RD BLACKBURN 382

133. *Brownhill, Whalley New Road 1908.* In 1776 a Petition was laid before Parliament to enclose some seventy acres of 'commons or tracts of waste ground' called Brownhill in the township of Little Harwood. The same year a Bill was presented for 'repairing and widening the road from Clitheroe to Salford Bridge, Blackburn.' Just to the left of the picture had stood the Brownhill toll gate. Until the arterial road was opened in October 1928, the only bridge over the railway was on Pleckgate Road; the four mile bypass from Yew Tree to Whitebirk, which today occupies the foreground, was built as a relief measure to find work for the unemployed. The cottages, on the right, were 'modernised' in 1915.

RISHTON COLLIERY

134. *Rishton Colliery circa 1910*. Coal was mined around Blackburn for over four centuries. Before the coming of the canal the coal mines of Darwen and Eccleshill exclusively supplied house fuel for Blackburn. In 1883 Mr. P.W. Pickup negotiated a lease for the unworked coalfield to the West of Rishton. This photograph shows the carts waiting to be loaded in the bay on the right whilst outside the manager's offices on the left are fully laden carts about to leave. Colliers can be seen on the steps which lead up to the cage. The colliery closed during World War 2 and only the offices, now converted into cottages, remain.

135. *Railway Road 1930*. The town's first news sheet, the 'Blackburn Mail', appeared in 1793. Many others followed including the 'Blackburn Alfred' (later the 'Standard'), the Tory reply to the Liberal 'Blackburn Gazette'. All had but a brief existence owing to severely limited circulation. In the 1830's the cost of each was 7d, and most were posted direct to wealthy subscribers. Only the 'Blackburn Times', founded in 1855, prospered; but it also has lately succumbed. The gates, right, led to Spring (Factory) Hill, which was the location of one of the town's oldest mills. Until recently part of Whitbread's brewery, the site is now occupied by the Lancashire Evening Telegraph which vacated its old building on the left. The bus is one of Ribble's Leyland Lions.

136. *River Blakewater, Water Street circa 1940.* The Blakewater was not always so polluted nor tranquil, some sixteen people having drowned in serious floods over the years. Charles Tiplady, the local diarist, recalled the pure brook he strolled beside 'along the fields to Brookhouse' around 1820. The traditional derivation of Blackburn, 'dark-coloured stream', seems at odds with this description. A counter suggestion, based on the Doomsday entry 'Blacheborne', is 'bleach-water'. Bleaching cloth was historically a tedious process of repeated immersion in water and exposure to the sun. Perhaps this was done on Blakeley Moor — a 'sloping meadow used for bleaching'? The river is now culverted and all trace of Water Street, left, and New Water Street, right, totally obliterated beneath the new Markets.

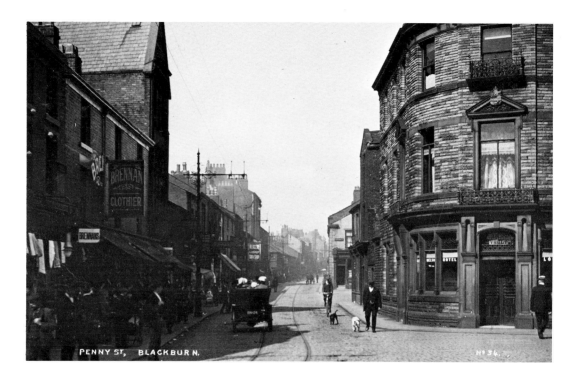

PENNY ST, BLACKBURN.

137. *Penny Street 1911.* Penny Street, supposedly named after the rent charge fixed on the building leases, had few houses of distinction. In 1868 it was the Irish quarter and the scene of a political riot. The Irishmen attacked the parading 'Brookhouse Lads' on their way home. The fray was quelled only by the intervention of the Mayor, the redoubtable 'Jackie' Smith, who threatened to have them 'shot like rapputs' if they did not disperse. No other remaining Blackburn street displays such marked change. The irregular buildings, left, have been replaced by a gleaming façade of concrete and glass. The road has been widened; the Lord Nelson (right) demolished. Only the Fleece Inn, beyond Starkie Street, occupies its original site.

138. *Darwen Street circa 1920.* The old market place was at the junction with Church Street — there being no through route towards Lord Street until King William Street was constructed in 1832. On market days the whole length of Darwen Street from Mill Lane to Church Street was lined with stalls where Victorian housewives in poke bonnets and crinolines replenished their household stores. The General Post Office, on the right, replaced the one in Lord Street in November 1907 though there was no formal opening ceremony as the Town Council was opposed to its character and situation. Beyond it — until demolished in 1978 — stood the Legs of Man, formerly the Paslew Arms, one of the oldest inns in Blackburn.

CHURCH STREET, BLACKBURN.

139. *Church Street 1930.* In 1902 the Old Bull was modernised for the owner Sir John Rutherford, baronet, brewer and one time Member of Parliament for Darwen. Its position as one of the area's leading hotels was confirmed. The doors finally closed on 8th April 1938 although it was not demolished until 1950. Gone, too, is the once familiar policeman on point duty at the junction. The fine Victorian façade, left, which included Thwaites Arcade, was demolished in 1971 to be replaced by the shopping precinct's austere wall — progress indeed! Church Street was widened and the skyline is now dominated by the brick tower of the Thwaites' brewery. The buildings, right, remain; only the Yorkshire Bank today occupies the same premises.

140. What better way to finish than with this fine aerial photograph taken in August 1920 by Aerofilms Ltd. It is amazing to reflect that as we look over Salford Bridge towards the Market Place with Preston New Road beyond, most of the buildings in this view have been demolished. The Town Hall and the not-quite-completed Public Halls are still with us; but the Theatre Royal, Reform Club, Thwaites Arcade, and the Market Hall — with its campanile clock-tower the symbol of them all — are gone. Just memories, nothing more!